The Truth About Hip ꞏꞏꞏ ꞏꞏꞏ

Forever

By Dr. Andrew Gorecki & Dr. Ben Fuson

# Table of Contents

# Why Read The Truth About Hip Pain?

This book was written for you, to help you live a healthier and happier life.

The human body is one of the most complex structures known to man, and it can be very difficult to find accurate and helpful information when your body is having a problem. This book is designed to simplify a complex topic known as *hip pain.*

As a hip -pain patient and sufferer for many years, and a physical therapist who now specializes in hip pain, I have a unique perspective that I attempt to share with you in this book. During my experiences, I learned that the more knowledge you have about your body and how it works, the easier it will be to live a healthier life.

If you're suffering with hip pain and feel like everyone else gets to live life and have fun while you're sitting on the sideline, read *How to Avoid a Hip Replacement—Naturally Without Medications, Injections, or Surgery.*

Use it. Gain Knowledge. Take control.

Yours in Health,

Andrew Gorecki

Physical Therapist

P.S. This book was written specifically for hip-pain sufferers looking to heal naturally without medications, injections, and surgery. If at any time while you are going through this book and don't understand something or if you have a question, please don't hesitate to email me directly andrewg@thesuperiortherapy.com

# Chapter 1: Life with Hip Pain

Being able to move around independently might be the purest form of freedom, yet many of us take it for granted. Life is movement, and movement is life. Without the ability to take one step forward each day, life begins to transform into a very isolated place.

Life changed for Ken and Sharon back in 2014. After thirty-six years of hard work and dedication, retirement was upon them. They had just finished celebrating with their friends and family at their retirement party. Ken and Sharon had been married for thirty-one years and had big plans when they achieved the summit called retirement. They had enjoyed many hobbies throughout their working years, but sailing was their favorite by far. It had been their dream to spend the entire summer on their beautiful thirty-six-foot sailboat on the Great Lakes. Ken had mapped out exactly what ports they would make, how many days they would visit each town, and he had even built in weather days to permit for a little bit of flexibility, as he called it, even though Ken might have been the most structured person I have ever met. They both had studied for years how to be the most efficient, safe, and enjoyable sailors they could be. It was time for them to finally live their dream.

Sailing is not exactly a passive hobby. It is a very active style of boating. It requires navigational skills as well as proper technique as it relates to aligning the sail constantly in the proper position in order to take advantage of the gift Mother Nature provides in energy through the wind. As Ken and Sharon were preparing for their summer-long voyage into the Great Lakes, Sharon began experiencing hip pain. This usually was after a long days' effort of preparing the boat for their voyage. Sometimes it was washing and waxing the boat that brought on the pain, and other days it was climbing in and out of the boat that left her in agony at night. Sharon had experienced some hip pain in the past few years, but it would usually resolve on its own in a few days and she was able to move on with whatever presented itself after a period of rest.

Sharon and Ken did what most of us would have done in this situation and made a visit to their primary care physician. They were relatively healthy people who were proactive, and knew that it wouldn't be a good idea to just ignore her hip pain while being gone on the lake for more than four months. They met with their trusted physician and discussed the situation. Sharon described that the more she moved each day, the hip pain seemed to increase. Activities like getting in and out of the boat, bending and squatting while washing the boat, and sometimes even standing or walking for long periods of time caused pain. Their physician instructed Sharon to begin taking an anti-inflammatory medication daily, and ordered an X-ray of the hip to see what was going on inside the joint.

Over the next six weeks, Sharon noticed that the medications helped relieve the hip pain and she was able to continue preparing for their summer-long trip without too much discomfort. The physician's office called a week or so after the appointment with the X-ray results, which indicated that Sharon had some signs of osteoarthritis in her hip and her physician would be referring her to a hip specialist. A few weeks later, Sharon met with the hip specialist, an orthopeadic surgeon with stellar credentials from the University of Michigan. After listening to Sharon discuss the activities that are causing her hip pain and reviewing her X-ray, he made the recommendation that Sharon get her hip replaced. He said there was not much you can do with a hip that has arthritis, therefore a hip replacement would be needed.

Taking the advice of the hip surgeon, Sharon scheduled her surgery for two weeks later. This was devastating news to both Ken and Sharon, because they would have to push their summer-long trip back by at least six weeks. They still kept the plans they had to sail the Great Lakes, but wouldn't be leaving the shoreline until mid-June of that summer. That still left them plenty of time to navigate the waters and see most of their favorite destinations. The thought of surgery was scary to both Ken and Sharon, but the surgeon reassured them that he had done thousands of hip replacements and she would recover just fine with no more pain.

Sharon went ahead and had her hip replacement and the surgery was successful. Sharon woke up from her hip replacement and was able to get up and walk that very same day. There was some pain, but Sharon was shocked at how fast she was able to get up. In fact, the physical therapy team came in within the first hour Sharon was awake and had her start moving her legs, moving her feet, and standing. All signs were that Sharon was on the path to recovery and would be sailing in no time.

About three days after her surgery, Sharon was at home and started to develop some pain in the area of her right calf muscle. The painful area was also very hot to the touch and red. Sharon called her surgeon's office to tell them of this new symptom, and they had her come in right away. Sharon had developed a blood clot in her leg, which is a common complication that occurs after surgeries due to the reduction in movement of the body and the subsequent pooling of blood that occurs in the veins due to lack of muscle contraction. Sharon was treated immediately with blood thinners and admitted to the hospital for observation. The blood clot was worse than originally thought and the blood thinning treatment did not seem to be working as expected. After ten days in the hospital with various treatments to resolve Sharon's blood clot, her leg became infected and the medical team had to amputate her leg in order to stop the spread of the infection. Sharon was left with an above-knee amputation.

After months of rehabilitation in the hospital, Sharon returned home at the end of the summer with a wheelchair to get around and her husband to care for her. Sharon and Ken's dreams of sailing the Great Lakes had sadly ended and their lives were forever changed.

## Chapter 2: Who This Book Is For and Is Not For

The story of Sharon and Ken is sad, but not uncommon. Research indicates that there is a 20 percent chance that there will be a serious complication during the care of a hip replacement. These complications include blood clots, pneumonia, and infection, among other things. Sharon's life was forever changed as a result of her hip being replaced.

In this book, I am going to explore ways to prevent the sad story that Ken and Sharon share with many others who undergo orthopedic surgeries. First, you need to understand if you are the right person to read this book. This book is not for everybody.

This book is for you if you are someone who thinks for themselves and does not follow advice blindly without researching all of the options. The reality is that most hip replacements are done because of two pieces of evidence: pain and an image showing osteoarthritis. This is despite the fact that we will discuss later in the book how many studies indicate that a large number of people are walking around with hip osteoarthritis without pain. In fact, 80 percent of sixty year olds are living without pain in their hip, but they do have arthritis. There needs to be more evidence to determine if a hip replacement is needed. Yet most people are told by their surgeon that they need a hip replacement without trying any of the other, conservative treatments, that are known to be effective. They blindly follow one of the most authoritative figures in our society without questioning. If this is you, then you probably won't like this book.

This book is for you if you believe the body can heal itself naturally. The reality of hip pain is that, regardless of the type of hip pain or diagnosis, all hip pain has a level of inflammation. Later in this book, we will talk about what inflammation is, but simply put it is the second phase of the healing process. That means that something was damaged that the body is trying to heal. Therefore, we should stop masking inflammation and pain, take a step back, and discover what went wrong in the first place that is causing the body to try to heal itself. If we fix that cause, then we will eliminate the inflammation and allow the body to heal itself naturally, which is what is has been designed to do since birth.

This book is for you if you want to find a natural solution to healing. If you are the type of person who is looking for a magic pill to fix your hip pain, then this book will be a waste of time. If you are looking for some fancy new device that magically fixes all hip pain, then this book will frustrate you. We will be discussing, in depth, the complex nature of the body, how it moves, and what goes wrong that causes hip pain in the first place. Then I will be offering solutions that are simple, prescriptive movements that you can do to fix the problem and avoid medications, injections, and surgery. This will provide you with a natural solution. My hope is that you are reading this book because that's what you want, hence the subtitle.

This book is for you if you have the desire to move again without pain. I believe movement is the greatest gift that we have been given. Without it, life becomes empty. I don't believe it is good enough to offer someone a solution to their hip pain without giving them back the ability to move again without pain. My hope is that by reading this book you will find not only a solution to your hip pain but also the ability to return to all of the activities that you love and that fill your life with joy.

This book is for you if you have the desire to be independent and not have to rely on others. One of the most depressing situations when you can't move because of pain is that you begin to need others to help you do things. That might be simple activities, like grocery shopping or working in the yard or house. As hip pain progresses, or if we end up having surgery, sometimes the dependency can start to include things like self-care and treatments that others have to do for us. My hope is to help you move away from being dependent on others and empower you to solve this problem yourself and learn the tools to continue to take control of your own health.

# Chapter 3: How Do I Know If I Can Help You?

I'm the owner of a physical therapy clinic in northern Michigan called Superior Physical Therapy. We serve more than 700 patients each week. We get amazing results, some of which you can read about toward the end of this book, as people were gracious enough to share their experiences. The reason we get such amazing results, among many things, is that we are very selective about who we work with. Let me explain myself, because I realize that might sound a bit abrasive.

When I first meet someone who is struggling with hip pain, I immediately listen to their story and take them through an examination in order to first answer one question. I want to know if the pain that they are experiencing is produced by a pattern of specific motions. Essentially, is their movement reproduced by some movements and then relieved with other movements. An example of this might be, "My hip hurts when I walk, but it doesn't when I sit down." If this is the case, this is a good thing. This means there are some movements that cause pain and others that don't. Ultimately, from my perspective as a movement specialist, if you can reproduce the pain with a pattern of motions then there is a good chance that you will be able to improve the motion in the other parts of the body that contribute to the painful motions, and this will relieve the stress in the hip. There is hope in this situation. This person is more likely to have success in our clinic. This person is also someone who can avoid a hip replacement, even if they have been told it is the only answer.

On the flip side is a person comes to me and states they have constant pain that never changes intensity, frequency, or degree, regardless of what activity they do. If I then take them through a movement examination and there is never a change in pain level no matter what direction they move, this is a tough situation. I use pain as a guide, or a lighthouse. Pain helps me understand where someone is successful and where they are not. As a movement expert, I know how to improve motion in any part of the body, but without pain as my lighthouse it becomes very hard to help someone improve. When someone is in constant pain that never changes, which is rare by the way, it also usually indicates they have a structural problem instead of a functional problem. Structural problems almost always warrant a surgeon to repair the structure. A high percentage of the time, functional problems can be improved by improving the function of the rest of the body. So there is a simple test: If your pain is reproducible, it is then reducible.

## Chapter 4: Two Types of Injuries

Think back to all of the injuries you've experienced in your life. Some may be sudden, and some may creep up over time, but they all change the way we go about our lives. All injuries fall into two categories: acute trauma and cumulative trauma.

Acute trauma means there was a moment in time when you knew exactly when you got hurt. The problem was immediate, and the trauma was at its highest level initially. As time went on, it got better. The other type of injury, which most people with hip pain have, is called a cumulative-trauma injury. Occasional pain started months or even years ago, now it is more frequent or constant. As time has gone on, instead of getting better on its own it has gradually become more of a problem. It is really that simple. There are two types of injuries.

Most people who are struggling with hip pain have a cumulative-trauma problem.

If you stay on the same path with a cumulative-trauma hip injury, inevitably it will get worse. The body cannot heal itself, because the stress or damage that the body is experiencing is still present and has increased over time, or accumulated. These are also called biomechanical problems. Another way of saying it is there is a movement problem. The more you move, the more injury you are doing to your body. It is accumulating. The tissue damage is increasing beyond what the body is able to do in repair at night when we sleep. The body is unable to keep up with the damage at this point.

If you continue to allow this situation to occur, you can expect that the list of things you cannot do to grow. At first you couldn't do strenuous activities because of your hip pain, like running, bike, walking long distances, carrying heavy objects around the house, yard work, or housework. As time went on, that list grew to include more things that you loved to do, like traveling, hiking, spending time with your family, playing with your grandkids, sitting, and eventually even sleeping. Since this is a cumulative trauma problem that increases when you move, the list of activities that you can no longer do because of pain will grow.

Movement or activity level is highly associated with sleep and mood. If you let the hip trauma cumulate over time, you would also expect your activity level to decrease, sleep to decrease, and ultimately your mood to get worse and worse. This poor mood will damage your relationships with others and isolate you from your friends and family. Not good.

More importantly, if you stay on the same path as mentioned before, you are more likely to suffer a major health event such as a stroke or heart attack and you won't even be around to share experiences with your friends and family. All because you let hip pain take over your life. You don't want this and neither do I, so let's switch gears here and talk about how you are going to conquer hip pain and change the path so that you have a bright future.

# Chapter 5: There Is a Bright Future

If you follow the process I'm going to lay out in this book, you have a bright future. I know for some of you that is hard to grasp, for various reasons. One reason might be the length of time the problem has been present. It seems that for every day, week, month, and year that our hips have been hurting, the more likely we are to not believe that the problem is going to go away. We start to have a closed mindset and self-talk that convinces ourselves that the problem is just how life is now by saying things like, *I'm just getting old, I've tried everything, and it still hurts*, or *I have arthritis and there is nothing that can be done*. All of these thought processes are self-limiting and allow us to forget one simple principle: The body heals itself when given the proper environment. That is a fact. Let me repeat: The body heals itself when given the proper environment. The length of time the problem has been there is not a factor in this equation. If the environment is still one that is keeping the healing process from progressing, we will continue to stay injured or unhealed. It has nothing to do with age, time, or genetics. The fact is that if we fix the problem that is causing the damage to the hip, the hip will heal itself. We must first believe that this is possible, otherwise the chances of it happening are much lower. I want you to have a bright future, therefore you must believe that it is possible.

Another major barrier for people dealing with hip pain is that they may have been told that they have arthritis and there is nothing that can be done except surgery. This causes them to stop trying other options. They have submitted to the fact that there is a solution out there (surgery), but they are unwilling to do it because of ... something. The reality of the situation, which we will discuss later, is that surgery is not the only answer. There are answers that provide many people with natural relief from their hip pain, you just need to educate yourself on what they are and have an open mind.

When people are suffering and in pain, this often has a negative affect on their relationships including their relationships with others. You see, when you are in regular pain, it affects how much we move and how much we sleep. Sleep and activity level are both strongly associated with our moods. When sleep and activity levels decrease, so does our mood. When we are in a bad mood, we tend to have poor relationships. When I was struggling with back pain and sciatica for more than a year, I became isolated from my friends and family. I was unable to participate in social events, and my world became small and depressing. Pain took over my life. The process I'm going to lay out will improve your relationships by indirectly improving your sleep, activity level, and ultimately your mood. Having a good mood will allow you to have deep, intimate, encouraging relationships with the people around you.

When you are struggling with pain during movement, the risk of developing a serious chronic health condition increases significantly. The top chronic diseases, which include heart disease, stroke, diabetes, obesity, and depression, all are associated with movement. The more we move, the less likely it is that these things will happen to us, and the less we move the higher the risk. Again, when I was struggling with more than a year of back pain and sciatica (which, by the way, were being caused by my lack of hip motion), I gained more than thirty-five pounds of fat. I was depressed. I was inactive because it hurt. I couldn't sleep because of the pain. I ate bad food to try to make myself feel better. If I hadn't found a solution to that problem, I would have developed at least one of the five major health issues I mentioned previously. If you follow my process, the future will have a lower risk of these scary things happening to you.

The brightest part of the future I'm going to lay out for you is that you can take control of your health and be empowered through education. This control over your health will allow you to save your money and time by decreasing the number of doctor's visits, medications, and surgeries that you likely will have if you stay on the same path. It will also increase your independence, because you will no longer rely on others for help. I believe independence is the brightest part of the future you will have by following my process. The worst part of my experience being injured for more than a year was that I relied on others every day for help to do simple things, like put on my shoes and socks. I relied on others to provide treatments to help me relieve my pain. I even relied on others to get the work that I was supposed to be doing done so that I didn't get kicked out of school.

You don't want to be dependent on others, you can take control of your own health.

## Chapter 6: The Single Biggest Mistake Hip Pain Sufferers Make

When you break down all of the problems and issues we are faced with in life, there are really only three ways to handle them. You can ignore them, alter them, or change them. Which one do you think we are all the best at?

Ignoring problems is what we do best. Think about the last time you noticed that your car tire was a little low on air. What did you do? Typically, you think, *That looks a little low on air*, and go about your day. You just ignored the problem. This cycle may continue for a week until you decide that you should put some air in the tire, but a week later it's low again and in the cycle repeats itself. You just altered the problem. Finally, you get tired of having to put air in the tire, and you take it to the shop because it keeps happening. The shop finds the problem isn't the tire at all, it's a bad seal, dirty rim, or leaky valve stem. You've finally changed the problem, but not before you caused some extra wear and tear on that tire.

We are great at ignoring our injuries. It really is simple to do, and something that we learned when we were children. Think about when little kids get a scrape or a bruise. When you go to look at how it's doing the next day, the area is already almost healed. From a young age, we are trained to ignore our injuries because they just get better. As we talked about before, the human body wants to heal and get better, it just takes a while longer and more effort as we age. We also alter our problems through use of braces, supports, devices, surgery, and medications. These things are just putting a temporary bandage over the issue, though, never truly fixing the problem. Finally, we realize that this problem isn't going away, and nothing is fixing it. We get fed up, realize that the suffering we are feeling isn't worth it and that we need to change the problem and find the real solution.

This is the path many have taken that has caused some extra wear and tear on the body, just like that tire took some extra wear and tear. However, I'm confident that because of your decision to pick up and read this book, you've decided it's time to change the problem and find the real solution.

# Chapter 7: Understanding the Healing Process

The healing process for any injury or pain is unique to the individual, as everyone heals at different rates. However, the human body is remarkable in creating a dynamic and automatic process incorporating many systems working together in order to heal. When an injury occurs, the body responds with what is sometimes referred to as *the cascade of healing*, a process that involves four phases.

## Phase 1: Hemostasis, Days One to Three

*Hemostasis* simply means stopping blood flow. During any injury, tissues become damaged, causing blood to flow out of the tissue and into surrounding areas. During this phase, the body releases chemicals near the site of the injury, beginning the acute inflammation cycle. These chemicals are called upon to tighten the blood vessels to decrease blood flow and to trigger enzymes in the blood to form clots around the injury, stopping the blood flow.

## Phase 2: Inflammation, Days Three to Twenty

The inflammation phase follows, and can last for several days while your body works to protect the area by destroying bacteria and removing debris from the injury site. During this phase, the body is preparing the area for the growth of new, healthy tissue.

White blood cells are part of the body's immune system and respond to threats to the natural equilibrium of the body. These types of white blood cells, called *neutrophils*, fight off potential infection to the injury site by removing harmful bacteria and fungus, and also by clearing damaged debris tissue from the area.

During this time, fluid from blood vessels leaks into the surrounding tissues, causing what we know as edema or swelling. This creates an area that can be warm, show redness in the skin, and become enlarged. This fluid also triggers the nerves in the area, as it takes up space that is normally not occupied by fluid. The nerves then send signals to the spinal cord and brain, causing one to experience pain, soreness, and sometimes even fever-like symptoms.

## Phase 3: Proliferation (Repair and Rebuild), Weeks Three to Six

When the injured site is cleaned out following the inflammation phase, the body begins to repair the injured area. Blood platelets release chemicals to attract cells to the area that begin producing a barrier around the injured area and also the collagen fibers that make up scar tissue. The length of this process of tissue repair will vary based on the location of the injury and the amount of blood flow to that area. Injuries to the hip joint will generally take longer to repair, as there is less blood supply to that area of the body.

## Phase 4: Remodeling or maturation, Week Six to Two Years

In this final phase of healing, the tissue slowly begins to mature and return to a level similar to its previous state. The collagen fibers initially laid down during phase three are arranged in a random order in the body's rush to heal the area. During phase four, those fibers reorganize in a fashion to support the action of the injured site. The maturation process cannot be complete without controlled stress to the injured area, allowing tissues to be stimulated to grow and improve function.

The healing process is an amazing act by the body that is natural and automatic, but it can be influenced by many factors including health, nutritional status, location of the injury, age, genetics, psychological, and medications or anti-inflammatory measures. Many factors are not easily controlled, but one factor that is controllable is the practice of continued, long-term use of anti-inflammatory measures during the healing process. Multiple studies have shown that use of non-steroidal anti-inflammatory drugs (NSAIDs) delays the healing process in musculoskeletal injuries. This delayed healing can lead to long-term problems and biomechanical dysfunctions, as the body will begin to compensate around an area of limitation, leading to further issues. So perhaps we should think about not taking anti-inflammatory drugs so often.

Take my friend and patient's example. We will call him Tim. Tim was a football player and quite good in his prime, and remaining active following his playing days kept him in good shape. However, about ten to fifteen years after his last football game, he began to have hip pain while at work for the postal service. His physician told him to rest and take some ibuprofen when he needed it for the pain. Tim began to take ibuprofen daily, needing more as time passed to help get him through the day delivering packages. It wasn't until his physician moved out of town and his new physician was getting to know him that his hip pain was brought up again. This time the physician suggested going to physical therapy and to limit his anti-inflammatory use.

Tim was just altering his pain, causing more damage to his hip complex with his long-term use of anti-inflammatory drugs. It was as if Tim had a balloon that got a hole in it, and he would fix the balloon by adding tape to the hole each day. As each day went by, that hole in the balloon tore a little bit more, creating a larger hole, and Tim would need more tape to fix the hole and stop it from leaking. Eventually, that balloon is going to burst and Tim will have a real problem on his hands. Thankfully, Tim was able to avoid this in his hip by finding a true solution for hip pain and allowing the healing process to fully occur.

See the following websites for more examples and a longer explanation of the healing process.

- o  http://www.shieldhealthcare.com/community/wound/2015/12/18/how-wounds-heal-the-4-main-phases-of-wound-healing/
- o  https://www.h-wave.com/blog/physiological-stages-healing-process-what-happens-when-you-injure-yourself/
- o  https://www.ismoc.net/nopillsnopain.html
- o  https://www.ncbi.nlm.nih.gov/pubmed/16476921
- o  https://www.ncbi.nlm.nih.gov/pubmed/3728782

# Chapter 8: What does my MRI or X-ray mean?

We've all had an X-ray or magnetic resonance image (MRI) in our lives at some point, usually due to some sort of injury or to find out what is going on in a joint or structure. The important thing to remember here is that you don't need an X-ray or MRI in order to fix your hip pain. This is a desire that we as therapists hear consistently from patients, yet it doesn't actually help us treat the pain more effectively! These images may, in fact, cause results to be worse for you, as they elicit fear, anxiety, and self-doubt that the issue can change. An image may show arthritis, narrowing of the joint space, bursitis, or a labral tear, all of which may be going on. However, what we need to realize is that these conditions are typically the result of a bigger problem. That problem isn't just your hips! It's the areas around the hips, which are not contributing to movement in the manner that they should, leading to increased stress in the hip complex and showing up as one of these dysfunctions. An image will give you a category or injury, but knowing that category isn't going to fix your hip problem and ultimately isn't going to guide your treatment.

Recently, I had the privilege of working with a gentleman who plows snow during the winter months. If you've ever done this task, specifically in a Northern Michigan winter, you would know that it can be a twenty-four-hour job and is done while sitting with a lot of twisting activity. After years of having this job, he began to have pain in his right hip. He went the typical route and saw his physician, had an X-ray (which showed bone on bone, but more on that later), was referred to a specialist, and was told that he needed to have a new right hip. Except he didn't want to go through hip-replacement surgery, as he was fifty-three years old. So, he sought out a different approach, attended one of our live workshops, and then had a consultation. He told me he couldn't fathom having to have his hip replaced when it hurts just when he is sitting and is worse when he has to back up when plowing. It turned out that his issue was more than just his hip, and he committed to trying physical therapy to naturally relieve his pain. We found his true issue was the lack of rotation in his thoracic spine. He was forcing his hip, which was already in a bent position from sitting, to take on undue stress when rotating to the right. Over the course of his therapy, we were able to improve his mobility and he began to complete multiple hours of plowing without pain in his right hip. It turns out he didn't need the hip replacement that his X-ray suggested.

Looking into the research on imaging of the hip paints an even murkier picture for the reliability of an image revealing a problem. A study titled "Prevalence of Femoroacetabular Impingement Imaging Findings in Asymptomatic Volunteers: A Systematic Review" offered the hypothesis that there would be very few individuals who had no symptoms with femoroacetabular impingement (FAI) or labral injury. What they found was, "FAI morphologic features and labral injuries are common in asymptomatic patients. Clinical decision-making should carefully analyze the association of patient history and physical examination with radiographic imaging." They reviewed 2,114 asymptomatic hips and found 37 percent with what is called a CAM deformity, 67 percent with a Pincer deformity, and 68.1 percent with a labral injury.[1] Cam deformities are due to loss of the sphericity (round shape) of this femoral head. As a result, the labrum can become "pinched" between the bone of the socket and the bone of the ball and is referred to as femoroacetabular impingement. All of these hip issues without any symptoms showed something deemed nefarious. In another study of 100 patients who were having hip surgery, it was found that 43 percent showed a labral tear in an MRI of their non-symptomatic (opposite side of the surgery) hip.[2] Both of these studies show that it is normal and natural to have an image that shows something abnormal, and a study by Brinjikji et al. shows that these percentages rise as the subject ages.

It is important to realize that these images do serve a purpose, but it isn't necessarily the purpose that you believe it to be. Will it help with a specific surgery? Absolutely, but it isn't going to help tell you what the treatment should be. In the end, imaging is a tool that is used when someone is about to have surgery, one that shows the surgeon exactly where to go in order to alter the hip structure. You should trust the health provider that you are working with, and if they don't feel you need an MRI or X-ray, then you should follow their advice. It may save you a lot of money and a lot of time in finding a permanent solution when the image is only going to place you in a category.

1. Frank, Jonathan M. et al. "Prevalence of Femoroacetabular Impingement Imaging Findings in Asymptomatic Volunteers:

A Systematic Review." *Arthroscopy,* Volume 31, Issue 6, pp. 1199 – 1204.

2.  Vahedi, Hamed MD; Aalirezaie, Arash MD; Azboy, Ibrahim MD; Daryoush, Tanine BA; Shahi, Alisina MD; and Parvizi, Javad MD. "Acetabular Labral Tears Are Common in Asymptomatic Contralateral Hips With Femoroacetabular Impingement." *Clinical Orthopaedics and Related Research.* FRCS May 2019, Volume 477, Issue 5, pp. 974-979.

# Chapter 9: Three Most Common Types of Hip Pain

The hips are a complex structure, and complex issues can occur with them. However, we are going to narrow it down to the three most common types of issues that I see clinically, and I will bet that most of the issues that concern you will fall into one of these as you read through this chapter. Hopefully you will be able to gain a better understanding of what you are going through.

The first type is hip bursitis. A bursa is a fluid-filled sac within the body that acts as a surface to reduce friction so parts of the body can glide against each other. There are 160 of these throughout the body, with the large ones located adjacent to tendons near the joints, where higher levels of stress may occur. Bursitis is a condition that occurs when these sacs become inflamed, which typically happens with repetitive or altered motions. Symptoms can include pain, swelling, and stiffness of the joint.

Hip bursitis usually refers to the trochanteric bursa that lies between the greater trochanter of the hip and the gluteus maximus muscle and IT band. See Figure 1.

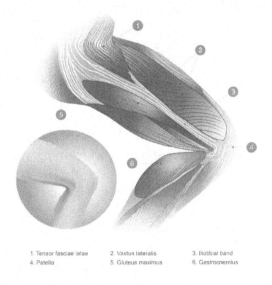

1. Tensor fasciae latae    2. Vastus lateralis    3. Iliotibial band
4. Patella    5. Gluteus maximus    6. Gastrocnemius

Figure 1: # 3 is the iliotibial band or IT Band which is a band of tendonis material that runs from the lateral aspect of the hip to the lateral aspect of the knee.

This is the textbook definition, but just think that this bursa is between the outside of your hip bone, near the joint and the muscles on the outside of your leg that run over top of it. The bursa is there to reduce stress, and stress here occurs with abnormal movement. See Figure 2. When the stress in this area increases, the bursa also has an increased stress response, or it becomes inflamed. This results in pain, which isn't the fault of the bursa itself, it is the fault of somewhere else moving poorly and creating an excess of tension in that area as it

36

compensates to complete the motion or the task. Treatment for bursitis directly through injection or surgery is only temporary, as over time the altered movement that created the stress is going to repeat the same story and you're back at square one.

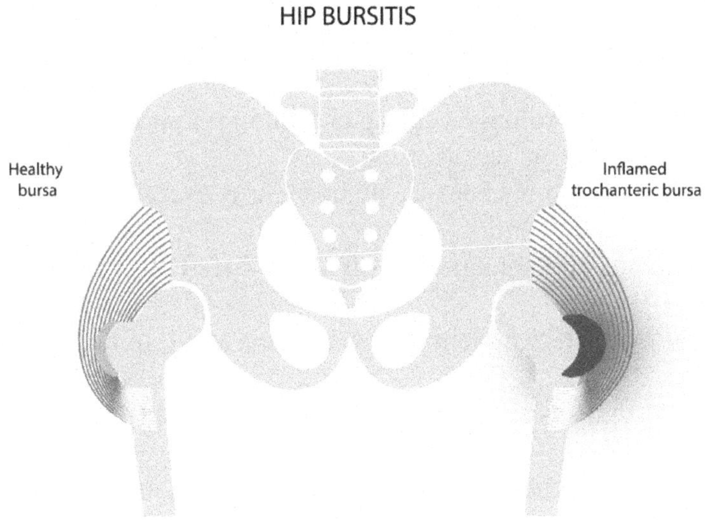

HIP BURSITIS

Figure 2: The hip bursa shown here is designed to provide lubrication between a tendon and a bone so that the tendon does not fray like a rope with movement.

The second type is a labral tear, which is damage to the cartilage ring (labrum) within the hip joint. The labrum is essentially a gasket where your femur and pelvis come together, providing extra stability and security for the joint. The labrum is tough tissue, but it may become injured with higher levels of stress. Often, injury is associated with repetitive motions.

Tearing to the labrum occurs when the tissue separates or pulls away from the socket within the hip. The resulting feeling is a deep ache in the front of your hip and groin area, a catching feeling within your hip, weakness or stiffness in the hip complex, and pain that increases with prolonged sitting or walking. Labral tears have a wide variety of symptoms because no one tear is exactly alike or reacts the same way as another since we all move differently. You may also have a labral tear and experience no symptoms at all. In fact, a study of people with no symptoms found that 38.6 percent of people with a mean age of twenty-six showed a labral tear on an MRI image[1]. This high number of labral tears without symptoms in young people demonstrates a high probability that labral tears are a normal part of wear and tear as we age. Further, a labral tear alone may not be causing the pain, and treating just the tear may be setting oneself up for disaster.

The third most common type of hip pain we see is osteoarthritis (OA), known more commonly as arthritis. This is commonly referred to as loss of cartilage, joint-space narrowing, bone spurs, or, most commonly, bone on bone. Arthritis has long been deemed a troubling diagnosis, something that is abnormal and has for years been considered something bad occurring within the joints of the body. Recently, additional research has found that arthritis is more prevalent and common that we once thought. Osteoarthritis affects 30 million Americans, 20 percent of the entire population[2], yet not everyone has symptoms. Also, a systematic review of 10,000 people showed that 80 percent of people over the age of sixty-three had an MRI indicating OA, yet only 13 percent had symptoms[3]. What this research tells us is that arthritis is a natural part of the aging process; it is as common as wrinkles on the skin or getting gray hairs. We have to remember that our entire being is aging and we see the external changes, but we don't see the internal changes that happen over time. Arthritis may not be the source of your pain, it may contribute to it, but it may have nothing to do with your hip pain.

1. Lee A. J. J., Armour P., Thind D., Coates M. H., and Kang A. C. L. "The prevalence of acetabular labral tears and associated pathology in a young asymptomatic population" *The Bone & Joint Journal.* 2015 97-B: 5, pp. 623-627.

2. Cross M, Smith E, Hoy D, Nolte S, Ackerman I, Fransen M, Bridgett L, Williams S, Guillemin F, Hill CL, Laslett LL, Jones G, Cicuttini F, Osborne R, Vos T, Buchbinder R, Woolf A, March L. "The global burden of hip and knee osteoarthritis: estimates from the global burden of disease 2010 study." *Annals of the Rheumatic Diseases.* (July 2014) 73 (7): pp. 1323–30.

# Chapter 10: Why Bone on Bone Is a Myth

Bone on bone may be the most common thing that people come into therapy for. They have been told they are bone on bone and they need surgery because there is no fix for this problem. I'm here to tell you that bone on bone, as we have come to know, it is not regularly happening. It may happen for a moment in time, but the body is not designed to do that. There is an issue causing bones to get too close to each other. Think about it like this: your femur and your pelvis are two rocks, and you strike them together with every step you take. In function, each heel strike causes two to three times your body weight to transfer through your hip, so if you weigh 200 pounds, you're striking those rocks together with 400 to 600 pounds of force. What do you think would happen to those rocks? Exactly, they would start to break and fragment apart where they are hitting each other with each step. Now, what would happen if you pushed those two rocks together and tried to move them? It would be almost impossible. The fact is that our body doesn't rely on its bony structure for support in normal function, and the bones are not meant to come together against each other.

Our bodies live for and crave movement, and this movement occurs in a tension-based structure. This means that our bones don't pass their load directly to each other, the forces flow through our fascial and muscle structure. Our bones float in this tension structure, creating a space between two bones and forming a joint. Fluid is within this joint space that allows for further ease of movement between two bones. Problems arise when this network of tension becomes weak, tight, or aligned incorrectly, causing the bones to come closer together. This means that in a weak, stiff, or imbalanced joint, the forces applied will pass through the bones or cartilage between them. This results in damage, inflammation, and pain due to the compression of the bones or other connective tissues.[1]

Can bone on bone be a real thing and an issue? Yes. Can correcting poor movement leading to approximation of bones eliminate the pain? Yes. Usually, bone on bone is diagnosed through X-rays taken with you in a static position at a specific moment in time, but you need to look fully at how the body moves in order to decipher the best approach moving forward and I can tell you that doesn't have to mean surgery.

1.  Scarr, Graham. *Biotensegrity: The Structural Basis of Life.* 2014.

# Chapter 11: The Three Most Common Causes of Hip Pain

So, if the type of hip pain isn't the cause, then what is actually causing the pain in your hip? Well, the obvious answer is that something is wrong with your hip itself, but finding what is wrong is the trickier part. The hip itself is a very dynamic joint and houses some of the strongest muscles in the body, but if those muscles are limited, they don't have length to move around and produce the force needed for function. These muscles need to be flexible and mobile in three planes of motion to accommodate the dynamic activity of the hip and produce the appropriate strength and stability required for everyday tasks. So, what is causing these muscles to be limited?

Each day we spend a lot of time sitting. Whether at work or at home, we sit to complete tasks, including reading this book! While we are sitting, we are causing a muscle in the front of our hips called the iliopsoas (or hip flexor) to shorten and become tight. This muscle attaches to our lumbar spine and to the inside upper portion of our leg bone. When this muscle is tight, it causes our back and our hips to work in a different way and become out of alignment, increasing the stress on the hip joint. This stress leads to increased inflammation and, ultimately, more wear and tear. This lack of mobility in a forward and backward direction can also occur in a side-to-side pattern as well as rotationally, making it very important that our hips themselves have good mobility to decrease the stress to the joint.

Another important influence on the hip is the foot and ankle complex. The foot is the first thing in the body to hit the ground when we're up and moving, has and there are many actions it must perform in order for our body to function correctly. When we're standing, walking, and taking steps, our foot must flatten into the ground and raise up in the middle creating an arch. This mobility is very important for producing the proper strength and stability of our hip complex. Go ahead and stand up and try these next movements to feel how this works. Try to flatten your foot into the ground, feeling the ground underneath the arch of your foot. Now move your foot in the other direction, shifting the weight to the outside of your foot so you're creating an arch in your foot. Now repeat that motion back and forth and think about what's going on in your hip. Is your hip moving? Yes! The hip is moving along with your foot and ankle. Another example is the toe in or out position of our foot and ankle. If we turn our toes in or out, the hip is moving to a new position as we do this. Why do either of these things matter to the hip? Well, going back to those big muscles of that hip, they need to work and they need to be turned on. One way to turn them on is to lengthen them. Having the mobility to toe in and also to flatten our foot causes the hip muscles to lengthen, leading to the ability for a stronger contraction. Or, simply put, they lead to greater strength and stability in our hip. Not only does proper mobility of our ankle lead to stronger muscles, but it leads to less stress to the hip complex itself. If we have limits in the mobility of our foot and ankle, or poor positioning, then the tissues of our hips are going to be over stressed. The stress and poor movement cause more pain and more compensations with our movement patterns.

A third area we need to look at is our trunk mobility, specifically the mid-back, which is a very mobile region of our body.

As we move around through our day, the mid-back moves with us, often directing motion to segments of our body above and below itself. One area it has a huge influence on is the hip complex. Try this sitting or standing, while holding this book in one hand. Take your free hand and reach as far across in front of you as you can and repeat it a couple times. Did you feel your hips move? Try it again if you didn't, because they are moving! Think about all the activity you do all day that includes reaching with your arms and moving your trunk. If your trunk doesn't move well, you're going to rely on other mobile regions to do that motion for you. One very mobile region is your hip complex, which will help by overexerting when your trunk isn't holding up its end of the movement bargain.

These three areas are the most common causes of increased hip pain and dysfunction with our daily tasks. The big takeaway here is that it is not always the hip itself causing the issues, it can be the hip reacting to other troublesome areas. The hip is responsible for many actions when we move around, both when sitting and standing. When another part of the chain isn't moving well, the hip is going to be left shorthanded and eventually will give in. The true culprits are usually not the obvious ones.

## Chapter 12: What Is Successful Treatment?

What if I could just get back to walking, hiking, sitting, laying down, golfing, playing pickle ball, kayaking, playing with the grandchildren, and moving without hip pain? (You can!) How could I achieve that success? (Find and fix the real problem!) Are anti-inflammatory drugs, injections, and surgery a path to success? (No!) These are all normal questions we ask ourselves when we are going through challenges with pain and mobility. There are solutions to get back to everything you want to without a high-risk procedure or medication, it's just going to take some work. So, what does successful treatment consist of?

The first step in successful treatment for you hip is having individualized care. Even though one person may have pain in the same area of the same hip the cause may not be the same. You have to have a plan that consists of finding and treating your individual deficits. In the physical therapy field we call non-individualized care "cookie cutter" PT, we should call it failed PT because with the one size fits all approach you'll never get to your true potential and achieve all the things that you want to do.

The second step in successful treatment is that it looks at the entire body, you must look at the areas around the hip to truly see what the issue is. A treatment plan can't consist of only looking at the area of pain and expecting long lasting and great results. Your provider needs to look at and test the other areas of the body including your foot and ankle and trunk to find the true deficit. Not finding this will almost always guarantee your pain returning in one way or another.

The third step in successful treatment is that it must be educational and empowering. You must know the why and how behind the treatment. You need to be educated on what isn't moving in your body and why that is causing your hip pain. Being educated not only gives you a higher level of understanding and the why behind the treatment, but it also allows for you to be more involved in your care since your level of understanding is higher than it was previously. This empowers you to know that you are getting to the root cause of your hip pain, allowing for better results and more commitment.

The fourth step in successful treatment is one on one care. When you go to a medical provider, specifically a physical therapist for treatment that care should be delivered by that physical therapist. You are paying very good money in order to get your hip pain fixed and you deserve to see the expert in the area the entire session, that expert is the physical therapist. When you go to a mill in which you get passed from therapist to tech, to another tech and then maybe back to the therapist that leads to disjointed and inconsistent care. Services to fix your problem should be delivered one on one from the medical provider.

The fifth step in successful treatment is hands on. Hands are like a second set of eyes for the physical therapist. They allow one to "see" through touch things that the eyes can't pick up. They also allow for guidance of proper mobility and movement during a task to help the patient's body get used to a new path of mobility.

The sixth step in successful treatment is it must be combined with movement and exercise. Treatment can't be passive. What are passive treatments? Anti-inflammatories, injections, and surgeries. Replacement is set to grow by 174% by 2030[1], with it becoming the go to and first option for treatment. But it alone won't end the pain and suffering because the movement dysfunction still lies underneath and hasn't been corrected, so once out of surgical pain you'll be right back to that pain you had previously. The way to correct the dysfunction is through movement and exercise so you can immerse yourself in the correct pathways and improve your overall mobility to avoid long term limitations.

1. Kurtz, S. (2007). "Projections of Primary and Revision Hip and Knee Arthroplasty in the United States from 2005 to 2030." *The Journal of Bone and Joint Surgery (American), 89(4)*, 780. doi:10.2106/jbjs.f.00222.

# Chapter 13: There Are Problems

Coming from two physical therapists this may be confusing to hear, but traditional physical therapy is not what it is going to take to fix your hip pain. That seems pretty wild to say after we spent years of study and a lot of money in order to obtain doctorates in physical therapy, but let's explain why.

Traditional physical therapy is what is taught to all physical therapists in graduate school. Now, while it provides a vast knowledge of human movement and lays the groundwork for full understanding of human movement, the traditional approach to therapy education is taught in segments. From the beginning of physical therapy school, you learn the human body in regions, studying the anatomy and physiology of that region before progressing to the next region of the body. One week you may be learning the foot and ankle and the next you may be learning about the neck. Traditionally, you are not taught that the foot may play an important role in how another region of the body functions. As we have learned, the cause of your pain is not always the area of your pain, so the true source of your pain may be missed.

In a traditional physical therapy setting, a physical therapist practicing this way may be able to give you ideas and instructions on ways to reduce your pain, which is helpful and needed, but falls short. You end up treating the symptoms and not the true dysfunction, making you rely on the physical therapist, massage therapist, or medication to manage your issue, and doesn't allow you to return to the activities you desire to perform without pain. Being reliant on something or someone to live a pain-free life does not sound appealing to me.

The underlying problem I'm getting at is that not all physical therapy is created equal, and it shouldn't be viewed as a commodity. Not all physical therapy is the same! Years ago, I stumbled into a course that taught applied functional science, which is a biomechanical-based way to look at how humans move through gravity in a functional manner, with the truth that the entire body functions together. Taking this course opened a whole new world to me in the physical therapy field, allowing me to help more people than I ever have before. It allowed me to ask the right questions to expand my knowledge, and you should be asking questions yourself when seeking help with your issue. Next time you're searching for a therapist, ask them these questions:

1. How many patients do you see with my specific problem?

2. Do you have statistics on the results that patients get from your treatments?

3. Do you have any literature from a peer-reviewed journal that supports your treatment approach?

Gone are the days when you could trust what you read on the Internet or in a magazine. You need to be your own advocate and seek out treatment that is going to address the true dysfunction and not just make you reliant on someone or something to treat the symptom.

## Chapter 14: How to Make a Change

Change is hard. No one likes change. It's a challenge that disrupts our routines and our level of comfort. But change is what needs to happen. We've discussed three ways to solve a problem, but if you have made it this far in the book, I would imagine that you are ready to truly solve your problem by making a change. So how do you take that next step to make a change?

Every year we have numerous appointments to address the various systems in our body. Form our teeth, eyes, heart, and prostate to our skin, we have checkups for our entire body … except one system. No one is testing our movement system regularly. And that seems a bit weird, because I would rather be able to move around in my day-to-day life than have pretty teeth. It also seems weird when you compare the musculoskeletal system to your teeth, because usually insurance covers musculoskeletal problems but not teeth problems, or at least not as good of coverage. It seems to me that if the statistics indicate that the second-most-common reason why someone uses the healthcare system is because of musculoskeletal pain, that we would have a better system in place for testing that system so that we could identify problems quickly and more efficiently than we are doing now.

The solution to this problem is to have a movement screening that is performed every three to six months. First, let me explain what a movement screening is. We have talked many times in this book about how hip pain is only a symptom of a bigger problem. Most commonly, the problem is that your hips, upper back, or feet are either not stable enough or don't have enough mobility. This poor motion above and below the hip complex causes stress and damage over time, ultimately leading to the symptom of hip pain. A movement screening must look at all of those areas and see how they move and how stable they are. Makes sense, right? Well there are a few different movement screenings out there, so let me talk about what makes a good movement screening. First of all, we must identify some truths or principles about the way we move:

- o We move in three planes of motion (front to back, side to side, rotate left and right)
- o We typically move when we are on our feet
- o If movement is what we are measuring, then movement must happen during the screening
- o The screening must look at the entire body, not just the symptomatic part of the body

A movement screening should be performed for anyone, whether they are in pain or not in pain. Ideally, a movement screening is performed when someone is not in pain so that we can prevent the pain from ever starting, but if you are in pain a movement screening is still the most important first step in identifying the permanent solution. I consider the gold standard of movement screens to be 3DMAPS, taught by the Gray Institute. This screening allows a physical therapist to assess how the entire body moves in three planes of motion in less than ten minutes. It identifies where you are successful and where you need help to be more successful. It is the movement screening that all of our therapists at Superior Physical Therapy are certified in. Other movement screenings assess someone in the sitting position, or lying on their back. I would argue that these are not as effective because the body moves differently when standing and fighting against gravity. Most of our movement problems occur when we are upright and moving around on our feet. I realize some patients have hip pain with sitting, and in that case I would absolutely assess someone's movement in the sitting position. But for the majority of people with hip pain, standing, walking, bending, and reaching are the most common problems.

The problem with treatments for the hip is that right from the start the focus is on your hip. The person examines your hip, with their hands, by asking you to move it, or via images. So right from the start, the healthcare provider is ignoring the rest of the body. It is ridiculous that we handle problems this way. It would be like if the dentist just drilled your cavity and said, "Have a nice day." The dentist would be irresponsible if she didn't tell you in the future to floss more to prevent this from happening or to recommend that you brush your teeth more. Imagine if dentists never recommended brushing or flossing, wouldn't that be insane? Imagine if the only time we went to the dentist was when we had pain and needed a cavity filled. Prevention is the most effective strategy.

So, it is my mission to encourage you if you haven't had one to get a movement screening on a regular basis, whether you're in pain or not, and whether you want to or not. Go and get it done. Schedule it right now. In fact, here is our clinic number so that you can take action: 231.944.6541. Simply say, "I want a Free Pain Relief Exam". We also see hundreds of patients online each year. If you would like to set up an online Pain relief Exam simply email

andrewg@thesuperiortherapy.com.

# Chapter 15: Success Stories

This chapter is dedicated to all of the friends we have met over the years. These are the people who came to see us when they were in pain and feeling hopeless, discouraged, afraid, and anxious. They were kind enough to share their experiences with you in the hopes that they can have an affect on your life.

"When I started here, I could barely walk with any pressure on my left side after I had my hip replaced. Andrew started me out and Nick finished my sessions at Superior PT for two months. I'm walking out the door today with a normal gait that is pain free. I am pleased with my progress and have a list of maintenance exercises to continue at home. Thank you!!"

—John Rowley

"I'm a lifelong runner. I came to Superior with my first injury: a painful hip. Sarah and Nick were incredible! After two months of therapy, the pain is gone and I can run again! Thank you!"

—Kerry Murdock

"I had damaged my right hamstring tendon doing a karate kick. The PTs at Superior were patient, attentive, careful, and knowledgeable. This was my first experience with physical therapy and it was very effective."

—Randall Hall

"I was referred by my doctor due to moderate arthritis in my right hip and severe arthritis in my lower spine. I couldn't walk or do everyday chores without horrible pain, and getting out of bed caused severe, hot pain. I slept in a recliner for weeks."

"I was evaluated by Brent on August 17, 2020, and started two sessions per week for five weeks on August 19, 2020."

"I worked with Taylor and Morgan most visits and met with Brent and Amanda for others. If something they had me do hurt too much, they would adapt it so there would be no pain. Most sessions they sent me home with a short video of a different exercise to do at home. I love this idea! I now have seven that I do every day, two to three times a day. Today, September 17, 2020, I walked out of my last session pain free and am back sleeping in my bed. Yay!"

"The whole staff is a pleasure to work with—from the friendly and knowledgeable front staff to the therapists and trainees. I will definitely recommend Superior Physical Therapy to everyone! And they'll be my first call if needed in the future! I can't say enough great things about them!"

—Lorelei Warren

"I am no stranger to Superior Physical Therapy. I battled foot problems, including foot surgery, for more than two years and the staff provided an inspiring experience. For the last three years, I have been running five to six days a week. I achieved a pace and distances that I never achieved in my life. So, in November a nagging hip pain that eventually forced me to stop running devastated me. I thought I had come so far in the last three years, but I even had pain with simple activities like stairs or sitting. I returned to Superior for help. Brent guided me to actively address my limited and asymmetrical flexibility as well as my weakness. Ben provided me additional insight reminding me how to better incorporate stretching into my daily routine. I very much appreciate their functional approach to pain-free movement and coaching me to return to running!"

—Kristy Burns

A

"Started with inner hip pain, but was discovered that the source of the problem was related to the IT band. Received several different exercises at different intervals to stretch and strengthen the muscles and core. Worked with three staff, all highly trained. Problem solved! I love the fact that after completing the program, I'm provided with a home program to stay in shape."

—Judy Izard

"Before PT: Right leg very weak due to prior knee damage, and follow-up arthroscopic surgery on right knee. PT experience, primarily with Mike with backup from Ben, was very good. The selection of exercises was widely varied and chosen to develop not only leg muscles and improve knee movements and strength but also improve hip rotation. Overall: Very good!"

—Dale Thiel

"Everyone at Superior has been wonderful! Working with Brooke and Ben has been helpful with my knee pain. I've learned lots of practices to take with me. I no longer have knee pain and have increased mobility in my ankles, knees, and hips. Thank you."

—Gina Limbocker

"My general experience here at Superior has been excellent. Courtesy and efficiency begins at the reception desk and continues through the entire forty-minute session. My hip/leg/balance issues were addressed with exercise and manipulation and I certainly feel stronger and better. The exercise was different than other PT treatment I received at other locales. The Tru-Stretch cage imparts a feeling of stability with its usage. Exercise practice with my own cane and ski-walking sticks gives me confidence in my own daily usage. Andrew was correct in assigning Mike Swinger as a very appropriate therapist for me."

—Jean Peterson

"I have ruptured left flank muscles from an auto accident seven years ago and now have severe scoliosis and a collapsing spine. I had trouble with my balance and with walking for any distance. Ben worked on my hip flexibility in preparation for spinal fusion surgery. He has been very personable and encouraging throughout my PT. The stretching has improved my balance. He had me moving every which way. I am sure that the therapy will help me recover substantially."

"I had fallen and sprained my left ankle and hurt my left hip and lower back. They helped me with stretches and gave me at-home exercises to work on. I do know that I have to keep doing them and appreciate the time and knowledge they gave me."

—Bryan Lucsy

"Overall I feel like I am moving better. I learned a lot about hip flexion, rotation, and overall stretching. I don't feel like my shoulder symptoms have improved, but my overall movement patterns have. Plus my shoulders and hips are in line again. I really enjoyed all the people, and overall atmosphere. They are an advance in technology and modern ways of thinking. It was a nice twist on regular physical therapy, a new way for me to think about my injury."

—Anna O'Hara

"Walking was difficult. It improved my leg, hip and back to make life good. Great staff."

—John Tisch

"Thank you very much, Ben and Keith (and Tim when he was here). When I started with you folks I had been dealing with bursitis in my right hip for nearly a year. It had caused me to have to cut back on my regular walking and yoga routines and, most troublesome, caused me to be awake many nights because lying down aggravated it. In combination with seeing Dr. Andriese, you folks have helped me regain so much of my flexibility and ability to move without pain (at least not too much). Ben and Keith are both terrific and creative in coming up with ways to help regain function. They were always good listeners and developed plans based on where I was at. I leave with clear instructions on how to continue this work at home. The whole staff (that I have encountered) at Superior are friendly and caring. I'll miss seeing you, but hope not to have to return! If I ever need PT again, however, you'll be my choice of providers!"

—Linda Ketterer

"When I started PT, I had intense lower back pain and some pain between my shoulder blades. I found the work in the cage to be very helpful and the exercises easily translated to do the work at home. Mike's descriptions of how the exercises were benefitting my back through encouraging hip movement helped me understand why being conscious of everyday moving would help. He was very kind and encouraging."

—Judy Macey

"I was having right hamstring pain for eighteen months when doing yoga. Therapy focused on stretching and strengthening three planes of motion, working on hips and adductors, too. Pain has resolved and I feel I have lots of resources to keep strengthening and stretching more evenly to prevent future problems. Super helpful!"

—Karen Lolas

"I couldn't be happier with my progress. After years of hip pain, I am now pain free, in alignment, and have a plan to maintain my hip health. Mike Swinger was an excellent therapist. He listened to my complaints, observed my movements, and put together a therapy framework that led to my recovery."

—Donna Stein-Harris

"I started therapy after having pain in my SI [sacro iliac] joint. Through therapy, this has improved immensely. I have learned a lot about my body and its mechanics. This includes the fact that a lot of the problems with my SI join were likely caused by my foot and lack of strength in my hip. Mike and Keith were great!! I am currently pain free."

"When I started with Superior PT, I had lower back pain and bursitis in my right hip. I also began to experience nerve pain down my right leg. Andrew discovered a huge knot in my right rear and started massage and exercises to relieve the pain. I am now pain free in all areas and have exercises to continue at home. The videos online are also great, since you can be sure you are doing the exercises correctly. I have been extremely pleased with my therapy and recommend all the therapists. Thank you so much. I can now enjoy walking and all the activities I have been unable to participate in lately. Thanks again!!"

—Pat Biegel

"Superior Physical Therapy has helped me understand proper foot biomechanics and how my body was designed to function. Stretching my hip abductors and loading my feet and hips has improved and pain has gone down a little. I hope that as I continue exercises at home that I have a lot more improvement."

—Joe Fordon

"It was great, very helpful. The back/hip exercises are reducing my back pain. Keith and Andrew were very pleasant and were easy to talk to. Thanks!"

—Gayle Esper

# Chapter 16: Top Three Exercises for Hip Pain

A few weeks ago, my six-year-old nephew was sleeping over at our house. I was awoken in the middle of the night by him exclaiming, "Uncle Joe, there's a monster underneath my bed!"

I went into his room and said, "Be nice to him and he'll be your best friend. Give him a pop tart or something." Okay, maybe I'm not the best uncle, but please read on.

The hip is like a monster underneath the bed, minus a few dust balls. If it's working correctly, it can be your best friend. It can assist far-away joints like the shoulder or ankle. Strength Coach Vern Gambetta called it, "The engine that drives the body." No wonder, as it has seventeen of the thickest, longest muscles of the body directly attached to it. But do not look for them, as they are superficially hidden by that big mattress we call the gluteus maximus. A few years back, researchers Porterfield & DeRosa discovered the monster even has tentacles! Well, sort of. We call it fascia. It functionally links the hips with pretty much the entire body.

This monster is tough, all right. It has a deep suction cup of an acetabulum, with a head of the femur as round as a bobble head, and a thick synovial joint capsule to seal the deal. How does the hip stack up to other monsters, like Godzilla? The hip's secret power is its contribution to three-dimensional loading (force reduction) and unloading (force production). Let's use the anterior cruciate ligament (ACL) of the knee as an example. Traditional rehab protocols have emphasized strengthening the quadriceps and hamstrings. However, physical therapist and bio mechanist Daniel Cipriani makes the point that these muscles only become protective as the knee flexion angle approaches ninety degrees. But now look upstairs at the extensive posterior hip musculature. By way of its multidirectional, multiplane orientation on the femur, it is well-designed to control the three-dimensional motion of the knee, with the most critical being internal rotation, adduction, and flexion.

Let's follow those tentacles up the kinetic chain to the shoulder. Can they protect the shoulder anterior instability that creates rotator cuff issues? You bet! Now we'll call on the infamous front butt, including the iliopsoas, abdominals, adductors, rectus, and so on.

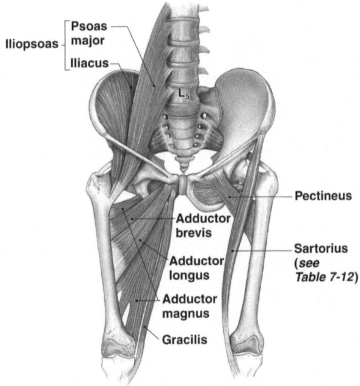

**(c) The Iliopsoas muscle and the adductor group**

Copyright © 2010 Pearson Education, Inc.

Try it yourself: Stand with your left foot behind your right foot with your right arm horizontally abducted at shoulder height with the elbow flexed. Feel the tug at the front of hips? This means they're locked and loaded to explode, and so are the abs by way of chain reaction between the hip and shoulder. Now turn the front butt off by sitting on it. Move the left arm to the right like you just did with the left arm. Feel the difference?

We make the monster happy when we feed it. No, not with sugary breakfast treats. Hips love ground reaction forces, gravity, mass, and momentum. They prefer lunges, squats, and step-ups. Adding some arm reaches in with the mix is like putting whipped cream on top.

They love variety in the form of direction, plane, speed, and load changes. However, be cautious about feeding the hips with empty calories. Many exercises performed in the prone, side-lying, or supine positions are what Dr. Gary Gray refers to as "isolated isolation." They turn off the hip's phone lines (proprioceptors) to the rest of the body and unhook those fascia links. They should be used sparingly.

Dormant daily living does not nourish the hip. Sitting and activities

that require prolonged static standing promotes injurious capsular

patterns. Interrupting these patterns with frequent snacks helps

reconnect those lines.

# Try These Top Three Exercises for Hip Pain

## Hip Flexor Stretch

How to do it:

1. Half kneel on a soft surface

2. Gently move hips forward and back, side to side, and rotate
   right and left for thirty seconds each

3. Repeat on other side

4. Repeat sequence two to three times per day

## Three-Dimensional Stepping

How to do it:

1. Step in each direction shown ten times

2. If balance is difficult, place hand on wall when stepping

3. Repeat sequence twice per day

## Groin Stretch

How to do it:

1. Place one foot on a chair, pointing forward

2. Other foot is perpendicular on the ground

3. Hold onto structure

4. Move hips gently toward chair until groin stretch is felt, hold

   for sixty second

These and other exercises to relieve pain are now available on our website in video format. Visit http://thesuperiortherapy.com/video-learning/

# Chapter 17: A Special Offer for You

To show you how much I appreciate you taking the time to read this book, I want to make you a special offer. I also know that you are dedicated to finding a solution to your hip pain and that you will do whatever it takes. You are motivated to find a natural way to heal your hip pain and you want to avoid or stop taking medications and injections. With all of that being said, I believe that I have a solution for you. I believe that nobody should have to live with hip pain. So this special offer is for you or anyone you know who might need help finding a permanent solution. I want to invite you to our private Hip Pain Relief Workshop. This workshop will answer any questions you have and allow you to learn even more about hip pain from the experts. To register for this workshop, simply call 231-944-6541.

If you have already been to the workshop or feel it would not be of interest to you, the second offer is to have a one-on-one consultation over the phone with me. Simply call my office at 231-944-6541, and I would be happy to spend some time with you answering any questions you might have.

I hope this book has helped you and that you will take action now to find a permanent solution to your hip pain. Thank you for reading.

## Chapter 18: Do This Next

The next step on your journey to pain-free hips is really simple. Stop ignoring your hip pain. Stop altering hip pain with medications, creams, and ointments, or avoiding the activities you love. Seek help from an expert. Call Superior Physical Therapy now for a free one-on-one hip-pain relief consultation at 231-944-6541.

## About the Authors

Andrew Gorecki received his doctorate in physical therapy from Central Michigan University in 2009, and his bachelor of exercise science degree from Northern Michigan University in 2006. He completed a fellowship in applied functional science in 2013 and is the founder of Superior Physical Therapy in Traverse City, Michigan. He and the rest of his staff specialize in hip-pain treatment. As a hip-pain specialist and previous hip-pain sufferer for many years, Andrew has a unique perspective, as he has received every treatment that is available. These ultimately failed, until he got to the root of the problem: his hips didn't move. Andrew is married to his lovely wife, Erin, and they have two young children, Max and Gibson. Andrew is dedicated to being the best husband, father, physical therapist, and friend that he can be and is here to serve. If you have any interest in reaching out to Andrew, he can be reached by emailing andrewg@thesuperiortherapy.com

Dr. Ben Fuson graduated from Michigan State University (Go Green!) in 2007 with a Bachelor's degree in Kinesiology and received his Doctorate in Physical Therapy from the University of Michigan-Flint in 2010. Ben is a fellow of Applied Functional Science, completing his 40-week fellowship in 2014, and is also a Certified Brain Injury Specialist. Dr. Fuson is a host of the radio show/podcase called Pain Free Living, speaks at educational masterclasses teaching people how to relieve hip pain, and is a hip pain specialist. Dr. Fuson was raised in Portage, MI and currently resides in Traverse City with his wife Megan and their dog Obie. In his free time he enjoys playing golf, mountain biking, hiking, and home improvement projects.